. . .

Flowers of Friendship

To My
Dear Friend

_____

From

_____

On

_____ 19 _____

Here are reflections beyond my ability
to express–
But from friend to friend I send them
with Godspeed–
The beauty and the glory of friendship.
Expressive? Yes!
But in my heart there's more unsaid.

. . .

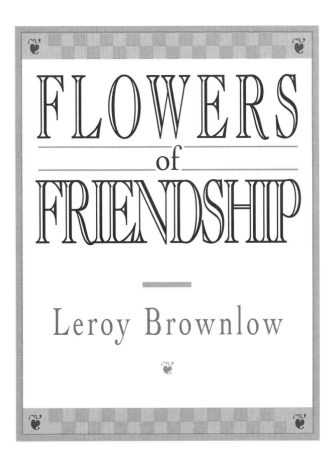

FLOWERS
of
FRIENDSHIP

Leroy Brownlow

Brownlow

Brownlow Publishing Company, Inc.

Brownlow Gift Books

A Father's World
A Few Hallelujahs for Your Ho-Hums
A Psalm in My Heart
As a Man Thinketh
Better Than Medicine—A Merry Heart
Children Won't Wait
Flowers for Mother
Flowers for You
Flowers That Never Fade
For Mom With Love
Give Us This Day
Grandpa Was a Preacher
Great Verses of the Bible
It's a One-derful Life
Jesus Wept
Just Between Friends
Leaves of Gold
Making the Most of Life
The Fruit of the Spirit
The Greatest Thing in the World
Thoughts of Gold—Wisdom for Living
Today and Forever
Today Is Mine
University of Hard Knocks

Contents

CHAPTER 1

A Sort of Divinity

FRIENDSHIP IS MORE PRECIOUS than gold. There is no one so poor that he is not rich if he has a friend; there is no one so rich that he is not poor without a friend.

It is not fancy imaginations or vain words, but rather the golden strand linking lives forged from untarnished mettle. It is like the rope mountain climbers use to bind themselves for safety and progress.

Real friendship is abiding. Like charity, it suffers long and is kind. Like love, vaunteth not itself, but pursues the even tenor of its way, unaffrighted by ill-report, loyal in adversity, the shining jewel of happy days.

Friendship is a gift, but it is also an acquirement.

It is a sort of Divinity which hovers over two hearts.

An Affinity Stronger Than Kinship

Friendship has been called the love without flowers or veils. It shelters like the outstretched branches of a full-leafed tree. Friendship preserves companionship. It is stronger than kindred. It is more generous than kindness. It has no savor of concession or patronage.

Wise men use the eyes of friends as lenses through which to better scan their horizon and more accurately chart the seas they sail. For "there is a power in love to divine another's destiny better than the other can, and by heroic encouragement hold him to his tasks."

Friendship is sincere. It scorns flattery. It faces facts. It is a lift. It soon stops when it is begun for an end. It is not a thing to be hurried. Rush it and it soon gets out of breath.

Like health, the wealth of friendship is seldom fully appraised until lost. Then its value floats before us like the vision in a mirage. The light of friendship is like the phosphorous in the sea, seen plainest when all about is dark.

Friendship is like a staunch ship, character built, so well balanced it rests evenly on its keel and rides all storms, a ship that is propelled by the heart, and piloted by the intellect.

Pure friendship is something which men of limited intellect seldom experience. As Samuel Johnson said:

> *Friendship, peculiar boon of Heaven,*
> *The noble mind's delight and pride,*
> *To men and angels only given,*
> *To all the lower world denied.*

—ADAPTED, R.L. JONES

A Friend Is A Person...

· *Who will help you in the hour of sickness;*

· *Who will help you up the hill when you are sliding down;*

· *Who will defend you in the hour when others speak evil of you;*

· *Who will believe in your innocence until you admit your guilt.*

· *Who will say behind your back what he says to your face;*

· *Who will shake hands with you wherever he meets you, even though you wear patches; and*

· *Who will do all these things without expecting any return.*

—DOROTHY C. RETSLOFF

The Hand of a Friend

I love a hand that meets mine own
With grasp of some sensation.

—MRS. F.S. OSGOOD

In Sunshine or Shadow

Friendship: Gentle as the dew from the silken skies, radiant as some glorious diadem, set with countless stars.

Friendship: Tried and true. Oh! How much you mean to those of earth.

Wealth may crumble like some shaken tower, but friendship still remains. Disaster and defeat may overtake us and, like a shadow, hide our star, and our ambitions turn to ashes on our lips; but friendship, like some guardian angel, rekindles and fans into life the hope which had almost fled.

When success crowns our efforts, friendship greets us with smiles and words of cheer, but with the same gentle hands lays the mantle of forgetfulness on the grave of our mistakes.

Thus through life, in sunshine or shadow, it bequeathes to us a constancy that never falters, a devotion that never fails.

—Yeoman Shield

CHAPTER 2

The Art of Friendship

THE NEED FOR FRIENDS IS IMPERATIVE. It is not good for us to be friendless. We were made to give and to receive, to help and to be helped, to encourage and to be encouraged—to feel a bond with others. Standing alone can never satisfy. Our nature requires a tie to faithful others. We call it friendship.

> *Without friends, no one would choose*
> *to live, though he had all other goods.*
>
> —ARISTOTLE

· *For life to be rich and fertile, it must be*
  reinforced with friendship.
    —It is the sap that preserves from blight and
      withering.
    —It is the sunshine that beckons the blossoming
      and fruitage.
    —It is the starlight dew that perfumes life with
      sweetness and besprinkles it with splendor.
    —It is the music-tide that sweeps the soul.
    —It is the victorious and blessed leader of
      integrity's forlorn hope.
    —It is the potent alchemy that transmutes

failure into success.
—It is the hidden manna that nourishes when
  all other sustenance fails.
—It is the voice that speaks to hopes all dead,
  "Because I live, ye shall live also."

For the loftiest friendships have no commercial element in them; to the contrary, they are founded on sacrifice. They neither expect nor desire gift for gift or service for service. No bushel of friendship for a bushel of favors.

Oh, how much stronger we feel when we know that amidst the tireless breaking of the billows on the sea of experience, there is no surer anchorage than a friendship that "beareth all things, believeth all things, hopeth all things."

—SARAH B. COOPER

Each friend represents a world in us,
a world possibly not born until they arrive,
and it is only by this meeting that a new world
is born.

—ANAIS NIN

· *Friendship develops because of mutual needs.* I need my friend and he needs me.

Acquaintances, however, are not especially needed. Consequently, if they drop out, we feel no sore loss for we never held together anyway. Breaking the tie with them severs no togetherness. It brings no loss of comfort, strength or help.

But with a friend it is different—when that tie snaps, we have lost our hold on that which we need and that which we clung. The loss is severe. The pain is sore. That is friendship. And that we long for.

Friendship is a needful bond.

—ANONYMOUS

· *As common travelers, we find friendship a sheltering tree. A rallying point. A refuge in storm. A shade from the blistering heat. A source of showering blessings that drop upon us. It is truly a strong, sturdy tree planted by the rivers of water that brings forth its fruit in a perpetual season.*

Friendship is a sheltering tree;
Oh the joys that come down shower-like.

—SAMUEL TAYLOR COLERIDGE

· *Friendship is a strong bond that takes time to form.* It comes gradually but surely when the necessary qualities exist.

We cannot tell the precise moment when friendship is formed. As in filling a vessel drop by drop, there is at least a drop which makes it run over; so in a series of kindnesses there is at least one which makes the heart run over.

—SAMUEL JOHNSON

· *Friendship is a precious bond that strengthens with cultivation.* Disuse may break it. Beautiful relationships don't grow through neglect. The wise man says, "He that hath friends must show himself friendly" (Proverbs 18:24); and Samuel Johnson used to say, "Keep your friendships in repair."

Keep your friend by not losing sight of him too long. Write when you can, remind him of yourself, and you shall hold the thread of his life.

Living well truly involves others.

> *For none of us liveth to himself,*
> *and no man dieth to himself.*
> —Romans 14:7

Furthermore, it requires that we keep the unfriendly things weeded out of the relationship. And that we be tolerant!

> *Friendship is a seed.*
> *Needs tendance. You must keep it free*
>   *from weed,*
> *Nor, if the tree has sometimes bitter fruit,*
> *Must you for this lay axe unto the root?*
> —W. Gilmore Simms

· *The first prerequisite to being a friend to others is that one be a friend to self.* The Bible speaks of "those that oppose themselves." But by being a friend to self, one makes himself worthy of friendship. He has the traits which cause others to seek a closeness with him.

A man who will not compromise himself can be counted on to be true to you; while the man who sells himself out is sure in a pinch to betray you. So the best friend is a person who is a friend to self.

Abraham Lincoln said, "I desire so to conduct the affairs of this administration that if at the end, when I come to lay down the reins of power, I have lost every other friend on earth, I shall at least have one friend left, and that friend shall be down inside me."

> *The Soul unto itself*
> *Is an imperial friend—*
> *Or the most agonizing Spy*
> *An enemy could send.*
> —EMILY DICKINSON

· *There is no surer way to make friends than to be one.* Hearts that have nothing to give find little to receive. Man reaps what he sows—or what he doesn't sow. If he sows friendship, he reaps friendship. And he should. Bread cast on the waters returns. On the other hand, no person should expect what he does not give. The law of sowing and reaping is so fair that all of nature abides by it. And so should I.

> *The only way to have a friend is to be one.*
> —RALPH WALDO EMERSON

· *Friendship cannot rise on the ladder of perfection.* Shortcomings and weaknesses are the common lot of us all. And this is one of the reasons we need each other. If we were perfect, the need would not be so urgent.

> *My friend is not perfect—no more am I—*
> *and so we suit each other admirably.*
> —ALEXANDER SMITH

> *Who seeks a friend without a fault*
> *remains without one.*
> —TURKISH SAYING

> *Two persons will not be friends long, if they*
> *cannot forgive each other's little failings.*
> —LA BRUYERE

> *If we say that we have no sin, we deceive*
> *ourselves, and the truth is not in us.*
> —1 JOHN 1:8

· *We are the most reckless spendthrifts if we let one friend drop off through inattention,* or let one push another away; or if we hold aloof from one because of petty jealousy or heedless slight.

Would you throw away a diamond because it pricked you? Yet one good friend is not to be weighed against the jewels of all the earth.

If there is coolness or unkindness between us, let us come face to face and have it out. Quick, before love grows cold.

The years...
Have taught some sweet,
*   some bitter lessons, none*
Wiser than this,—to spend in all things else,
But of old friends to be most miserly.
                    —JAMES RUSSELL LOWELL

· *A friend is helpful in time of need:* When your heart bleeds, he weeps with you. When you fall, his hand is stretched out to lift you up. When your goods run out, he shares with you.

And all because he is a friend!

So there is one nice thing about need—it reveals your friends.

But in deed,
A friend is never known
*   till a man have need.*
                    —JOHN HEYWOOD

He is a friend who, in dubious circumstances,
aids in deeds when deeds are necessary.
                    —PLAUTUS

· *A friend rouses our spirits in time of adversity.* Among the friends of Paul the apostle, no doubt many were afraid and ashamed. Paul was a prisoner. Times were hard. And doubtless the tie of friendship with many broke under the pull of fear and disgrace. But there was one upon whom he could count. One the world's enmity and contempt never affected. The probability of being thrown to wild beasts in the arena, or cast into a pot of boiling oil, or nailed to a cross, never strained his loyalty. That friend's name was Onesiphorus. He never faltered.

And Paul's expression of appreciation of him stands out as one of literature's classics:

> *The Lord give mercy unto the house of*
> *Onesiphorus; for he oft refreshed me, and*
> *was not ashamed of my chain.*
> —II TIMOTHY 1:16

· *Friends can talk.* The precious tie between them allows them to talk—even when angered; and their talking gives understanding, quiets the wrath, and forges stronger links of love.

> *I was angry with my friend:*
> *I told my wrath, my wrath did end.*
> *I was angry with my foe:*
> *I told it not, my wrath did grow*
> *A Poison Tree.*
> —WILLIAM BLAKE

· *A friend's sympathy–Ah! that's what we need.* It cheers. It helps to right seeing. It heals. It strengthens. It exalts and brings one nearer to God. It quickens not the worst things but the best things in a man. It has in it always a pulse of heavenly love. It never aggravates a bad symptom. It never accelerates a wicked course. It stills the troubled waters. It rests and soothes the aching heart. It takes one forward into companionships which are above the stars. It is more palatable than food; it is more refreshing than light; it is more fragrant than flowers; it is sweeter than songs.

–F.A. NOBLE

Rejoice with them that do rejoice, and weep with them that weep.
–ROMANS 12:15

· *In the understanding link of friendship there is a heart language too great for tongue or ear.* No tongue can speak it. No ear can hear it. We comprehend it with the heart. We see and hear what our friend meant–not just what he said, not just what he did. It is a kind of communication beyond the common forms.

The language of friendship is not words,but meanings. It is an intelligence above language.
–HENRY DAVID THOREAU

Treat your friends for what you know them to be. Regard no surfaces, consider not what they did, but what they intended.
–HENRY DAVID THOREAU

· *A friend does not judge another.* Rather than judge you, he tolerates you and apologizes for you. There is more mercy in his heart than censure. He never tries to elevate himself by stepping on you.

> *My friend, judge not me,*
> *Thou seest I judge not thee.*
> —WILLIAM CAMDEN

> *Judge not that ye be not judged.*
> —MATTHEW 7:1

· *A friend rejoices with us in our successes.* Mark Twain said, "When you ascend the hill of prosperity may you not meet a friend." But Twain was a humorist and the statement was given in jest. It applies only to acquaintances—not true friends. A friend loves, and "love envieth not."

Misfortune tests our friends. But so does prosperity.

> *The shifts of fortune*
> *test the reliability of friends.*
> —CICERO

· *True friends have no solitary joys or sorrows.* Both are shared. In the hour of peace and gladness, what is our want? Friendship. When our hearts overflow with gratitude, what is our need? A friend. When distress haunts us and misery walks by our side, where do we turn? To friends. When our hearts bleed and our sacred emotion finds no utterance, what does our heart long for? Friends. Friends to share. Friends to bear.

Two are better than one.
—ECCLESIASTES 4:9

· *Friends are too valuable not to hold them close to the soul.* That being where they belong, we should do more than keep a precious place reserved for them—we should grip them with our love, thoughtfulness and gratitude. They can be held. For the right kind of people are not apt to pull away from a person who demonstrates that he is on their side.

Those friends thou has and their
*   adoption tried*
Grapple them to thy soul
*   with hoops of steel.*
—SHAKESPEARE

· *We have a way of knowing our friends.* Their words. Their deeds. Their gestures. Just like a tree is known by its fruits. And this is no major accomplishment, for even a dog can soon tell a friend.

Nature teaches beasts to know their friends.
—SHAKESPEARE

· *How good it is to have friends around.* We are so constituted that we do not enjoy the life of a hermit. We need associates. Our hearts yearn for communion with a like-minded heart. It is essential to happiness.

> *Happy is the house that shelters a friend.*
> —RALPH WALDO EMERSON

· *If beauty is as beauty does, then good friends are the best beauty treatment.* They are because they cultivate the beautiful within us.

Mrs. Browning the poet said to Charles Kingsley the novelist, "What is the secret of your life? Tell me, that I may make mine beautiful also."

Thinking a moment, the beloved old author replied, "I had a friend."

A friend—true and honorable—has that effect. He has qualities which rub off on us.

> *Know ye not that a little leaven*
> *leaveneth the whole lump?*
> —I CORINTHIANS 5:6

· *Old friends are best.* They have proved themselves. There have been enough circumstances to test them, and their loyalty is unquestioned. Of course, some new ones have aged and ripened mighty fast, so fast that we consider them old though they are new, as we count days.

Yes'm old friends is always best,
'less you can catch a new one
that's fit to make an old one out of.
—SARAH ORNE JEWETT

· *Birth gives us our relatives, but choice gives us our friends.* Fate will not let us pick our relatives, but we are allowed to select our friends. So if we don't have the right friends, it is because we made the wrong choices or pursued the wrong courses. No one to blame but ourselves. Thus we should be slow in choosing a friend, and much slower in changing.

Fate chooses our relatives,
we choose our friends.
—JACQUES DELILLE

· *Having a friend makes one indispensable.* Each needs the other—to love and be loved, to serve and be served. So just as long as you have a friend, you have a vital role in society; and what sweet satisfaction there is in being needed.

So long as we love we serve; so long as
we are loved by others, I would almost say
that we are indispensable; and no man is
useless while he has a friend.

—ROBERT LOUIS STEVENSON

CHAPTER 3

Said in Few Words

FRIENDSHIP IS A CHAIN OF GOLD...Shaped in God's all perfect mold...Each link a smile, a laugh,a tear...A grip of the hand, a word of cheer...Steadfast as the ages roll...Binding closer soul to soul...No matter how far or heavy the load...Sweet is the journey on friendship's road.

—AUTHOR UNKNOWN

A friend has the skill and observation of the best physician; the diligence and vigilance of the best nurse; and the tenderness and patience of the best mother.

—CLARENDON

They are rich who have friends.

—SCANDINAVIAN PROVERB

Faithful are the wounds of a friend; but the kisses of an enemy are deceitful.

—BIBLE

Go often to the house of thy friend, for weeds choke up the unused path.

—SCANDINAVIAN PROVERB

*True friendship is no gourd, springing
in a night and withering in a day.*
—CHARLOTTE BRONTE

*The friendship of the good, and of those who
have the same virtues, is perfect friendship.
Such friendships, therefore, endure so long as
each retains his character and virtue is
a lasting thing.*
—ARISTOTLE

*To have a friend is to have one of the sweetest
gifts that life can bring; to be a friend is to
have a solemn and tender education of soul
from day to day.*
—AMY ROBERTSON BROWN

GIVE ME A FEW FRIENDS who will love me for
what I am, or am not, and keep ever burning before my
wondering steps the kindly light of hope. And though
age and infirmity overtake me, and I come not in sight
of the castle of my dreams; teach me still to be thankful
for life and time's old memories that are good and
sweet. And may the evening twilight find me gentle still.
—AUTHOR UNKNOWN

*Make no friendship with an angry man;
and with a furious man thou shalt not go.*
—BIBLE

WHEN GOOD FRIENDS WALK BESIDE US...On the trails that we must keep...Our burdens seem less heavy... And the hills are not so steep...The weary miles pass swiftly...Taken in a joyous stride...And all the world seems brighter...When friends walk by our side.

—AUTHOR UNKNOWN

Friendship renders prosperity more brilliant, while it lightens adversity by sharing it and making its burdens common.
—CICERO

TO BE UNSELFISH in everything, especially in love and friendship, was my highest pleasure, my maxim, my discipline.

—GOETHE

In pure friendship there is a sensation of felicity which only the well-bred can attain.
—LA BRUYERE

OF ALL HAPPINESSES, the most charming is that of a firm and gentle friendship. It sweetens all our cares, dispels our sorrows, and counsels us in all extremities. Nay, if there were no other comfort in it than the bare exercise of so generous a virtue, even for that single reason a man would not be without it.

—SENECA

OTHER BLESSINGS may be taken away, but if we have acquired a good friend by goodness, we have a blessing which improves in value when others fail. It is even heightened by sufferings.

—W.E. CHANNING

FRIENDSHIP THAT FOLLOWS from the heart cannot be frozen by adversity, as the water that flows from the spring cannot congeal in winter.

—JAMES FENIMORE COOPER

Something like home that is not home is to be desired, it is found in the house of a friend.

—SIR W. TEMPLE

FRIENDSHIP HATH THE SKILL and observance of the best physician; the diligence and vigilance of the best nurse; and the tenderness and patience of the best mother.

—LORD CLARENDON

Life hath no blessing like a prudent friend.

—EURIPIDES

Friends are in life's exchange the sterling coin,
True tender for the rarest forms of joy:
The only pauper is the friendless man.

—ANONYMOUS

CHAPTER 4

Decorated With Friends

*Y*OUR HOUSE WILL LOOK BETTER, if you decorate it with friends. They are the ornaments that will give it more attraction and cheer than all others combined. Nothing is comparable to the living ornaments that breathe so much warmth into plain quarters.

Grandmother's little farm house was a classic example. I have a picture of that old place, but I have a clearer picture in my album of precious memories. That little humble abode was inexpensive and unpretentious. No plumbing. No electricity. Only one carpet she made by hand. But it had a big cook stove and a big dining table. It was a common practice for her house to be adorned with the unexcelled beauty of pleasant friends. When I was a child we went there almost every Sunday. There was love. There was joy. It was there that we experienced the spirit-lifting feeling that lumber and nails, brick and mortar, can never give. It had what mansions often lack—love! friendship! That country home had a touch of warm, pulsating beauty that only people can give four walls. The warmth and joy I found there made it a place of priceless attraction.

A Rose to the Living

A rose to the living is more
Than sumptuous wreaths to the dead;
In filling love's infinite store,
A rose to the living is more,
If graciously given before
The hungering spirit is fled—
A rose to the living is more
Than sumptuous wreaths to the dead.

—Nixon Waterman

The ornament of a house
is the friends that frequent it.

—Ralph Waldo Emerson

House by the Side of the Road

Let me live in a house by the side of the road
Where the race of men go by—
The men who are good and the men who
   are bad,
As good and as bad as I.
I know there are brook-gladdened
   meadows ahead,
And mountains of wearisome height;
That the road passes on through the long
   afternoon,
And stretches away to the night.
And still I rejoice when the travelers rejoice
And weep with the strangers that moan,
As I live in my house by the side of the road
And be a friend to man.

—SAM WALTER FOSS

No Fickle Shadow

THE SHADOW ONCE SAID to its fellow-traveler: "No one is a friend like me. I follow you every step of the way. When you stand I am close by. When you walk I walk with you. When you run I keep stride with you. I am your constant companion. In sunlight or in moonlight I never forsake you."

The Body answered: "Yes, you go with me in sunlight and in moonlight. But where are you when neither the sun nor the moon shines upon me?"

A true friend, however, is no fickle shadow. His constancy is not dependent on fair weather. His love is higher than the clouds. His relationship with you is governed by that which is within him—not exterior circumstances. Consequently, he will stick with you when the earth shakes and trembles and the storm clouds blot out the sun, the moon and the stars.

In olden times John Huss had such a friend. When he was on his way to the stake to be burned, an old friend stepped out from among the sightseers and gripped his hand without saying a word. Huss turned and said that only God and himself knew how much that handclasp meant in the painful hour.

Such a friend is our stay in life and in death.

Thus, God's bright sunshine overhead,
God's flowers beside your feet,
The path of life that you must tread
Can little hold of fear or dread;
And by such pleasant pathways led,
May all your life be sweet.

HELEN WAITHMAN

The violet loves a sunny bank,
The cowslip loves the lea,
The scarlet creeper loves the elm;
But I love thee.

Violets, shy violets!
How many hearts with thee compare,
Who hide themselves in thickest green,
And thence unseen
Ravish the enraptured air
With sweetness, dewy, fresh and rare!
Violets, shy violets!
Human hearts to me shall be
Viewless violets in the grass,
And as I pass,
Odour and sweet imagery
Will wait on mine and gladden me.

GEORGE MEREDITH

CHAPTER 5

On Friendship

I AWOKE THIS MORNING with devout thanksgiving for my friends, the old and the new. I am not so ungrateful as not to see the wise, the lovely and the noble-minded as from time to time they pass my gate. Who hears me, who understands me, becomes mine—a possession for all time. Nor is Nature so poor but she gives me this joy several times, and thus we weave social threads of our own, a new web of relations; and we shall by and by stand in a new world of our own creation, and no longer strangers and pilgrims in a traditionary globe.

Friendship, like the immortality of the soul, is too good to be believed. When friendships are real, they are not glass threads or frostwork, but the solidest thing we know. The sweet sincerity of joy and peace which I draw from the alliance with my brother's soul is the kernel itself whereof all nature and all thought is but the husk and shell. Happy is the house that shelters a friend!

There are two elements that go into the composition of friendship, each so sovereign that I can detect no superiority in either, no reason why either should be first named. One is *truth*. A friend is a person with whom I may be sincere. Before him I may think aloud. I may deal with him with the simplicity and wholeness with which one chemical atom meets another. Sincerity is the luxury allowed, being permitted to speak truth, as having none above it to court or conform unto.

The other element of friendship is *tenderness*. We are holden to men by every sort of tie, by blood, by pride, by fear, by hope, by lucre, by lust, by hate, by admiration, by every circumstance and badge and trifle—but we can scarce believe that so much character can subsist in another as to draw us by love. Can another be so blessed and we so pure that we can offer him tenderness? When a man becomes dear to me I have touched the goal of fortune.

I wish that friendship should have feet, as well as eyes and eloquence. It must plant itself on the ground, before it vaults over the moon. I wish it to be a little of a citizen, before it is quite a cherub. We chide the citizen because he makes love a commodity. As such, it is an exchange of gifts, of useful loans; it is good neighborhood; it watches with the sick; it holds the pall at the funeral; and quite loses sight of the delicacies and nobility of the relation. I hate the prostitution of the name of friendship to signify modish and worldly alliances. I much prefer the company of ploughboys and tin-peddlers to the silken and perfumed amity which celebrates its days of encounter by a frivolous display.

The end of friendship is a commerce the most strict and homely that can be joined; more strict than any of which we have experienced. It is for aid and comfort through all the relations and passages of life and death. It is fit for serene days and graceful gifts and country rambles, but also for rough roads and hard fare, shipwreck, poverty and persecution. We are to dignify to each other the daily needs and offices of man's life, and embellish it by courage, wisdom and unity. It should never fall into something usual and settled, but should be alert and inventive and add rhyme and reason to what was drudgery.

But let me alone to the end of the world, rather than that my friend should overstep, by a word or a look, his real sympathy. I am equally balked by antagonism and by compliance. *Let him not cease an instant to be himself.* The only joy I have in his being mine, is that the *not mine* is *mine.* I hate where I look for a manly furtherance or at least a manly resistance, to find a mush of concession. Better be a nettle in the side of your friend than his echo. There must be very two, before there can be very one.

Understandably, he only is fit for friendship who is magnanimous. Therefore, treat you friend as a spectacle. Of course he has merits that are not yours, and that you cannot honor if you must needs hold him too close to your person. Stand aside; give those merits room; let them mount and expand. Are you the friend of your friend's buttons, or of his thoughts?

Remember—we must be our own before we can be another's. The least defect of self-possession vitiates, in my judgment, the entire relation.

So we hasten to say—what is so great as friendship, let us carry with what grandeur of spirit we can. For the only way to have a friend is to be one.

The higher the style we demand of friendship, of course the less easy to establish it with flesh and blood. Only be admonished by what you already see, not to strike leagues of friendship with cheap persons, where no friendship can be. Our impatience betrays us into rash and foolish alliances. But by persisting in your path, though you forfeit the little you gain the great. You demonstrate yourself, so as to put yourself out of the reach of false relations, and you draw to you the first-born of the world.

—RALPH WALDO EMERSON
(ABRIDGED)

CHAPTER 6

A Friend Is

The most I can do for my friend is simply to be his friend. I have no wealth to bestow upon him. If he knows that I am happy in loving him he will want no other reward. Is not friendship divine in this?
—LAVATIN

You must therefore, love me, myself, and not my circumstances, if we are to be real friends.
—CICERO

Animals are such agreeable friends, they ask no questions, they pass no criticisms.
—GEORGE ELIOT

No life is so strong and complete, But it yearns for the smile of a friend.
—WALLACE BRUCE

True friendship comes when silence between two people is comfortable.
—DAVE TYSON GENTRY

You can always tell a real friend: when you've made a fool of yourself, he doesn't feel you've done a permanent job.
—LAURENCE J. PETER

Instead of loving your enemies, treat your friends a little better.
—ED HOWE

One friend in a lifetime is much; two are many; three are hardly possible.
—HENRY ADAMS

Do not use a hatchet to remove a fly from your friend's forehead.
—CHINESE PROVERB

The best rule of friendship is to keep your heart a little softer than your head.
—GEORGE SANTAYANA

Friendship is a word, the very sight of which in print makes the heart warm.
—AUGUSTINE BIRRELL

I would not live without the love of my friends.
—JOHN KEATS

*The comfort of having a friend may be
taken away, but not that of having had one.*
—SENECA

*A friend is the gift of God,
and He only who made hearts
can unite them.*
—SOUTHEY

*Learn to greet your friends with a smile;
they carry too many frowns in their own
hearts to be bothered with yours.*
—MARY ALLETTE AYER

Friendship is the greatest luxury of life.
—EDWARD EVERETT HALE

*Be slow in choosing a friend,
slower in changing.*
—BENJAMIN FRANKLIN

*There is no folly equal to that of
throwing away friendship,
in a world where friendship is so rare.*
—BULWER-LYTON

Friendship is love without wings.
—BYRON

Two friends, two bodies with one soul inspired.
—ALEXANDER POPE

There are no rules of friendship; it must be left to itself; we cannot force it any more than love.
—HAZLITT

We can never replace a friend.
When a man is fortunate enough to have several, he finds they are all different; no one has a double in friendship.
—SCHILLER

Friendship is the marriage of the soul.

All who would win joy, must share it; happiness was born a twin.
—LORD BYRON

A friend is, as it were, a second self.
—CICERO

Hold a true friend with both your hands.
—NIGERIAN PROVERB

I no doubt deserved my enemies, but I don't believe I deserved my friends.
—WALT WHITMAN

*Traveling in the company of those we love
is home in motion.*
—LEIGH HUNT

*Friendship is always a sweet responsibility,
never an opportunity.*
—KAHIL GIBRAN

*Friendship consists in forgetting what one gives
and remembering what one receives.*
—ALEXANDRE DUMAS THE YOUNGER

*Friendship improves happiness,
and abates misery, by doubling our joy,
and dividing our grief.*
—JOSEPH ADDISON

*The better part of one's life
consists of his friendships.*
—ABRAHAM LINCOLN

*If a man does not make new acquaintances
as he advances through life, he will soon find
himself left alone. A man, sir, should keep his
friendship in a constant repair.*
—SAMUEL JOHNSON

Friendship is love with understanding.
—ANCIENT PROVERB

CHAPTER 7

In Tune

I don't remember when I first began
To call you "friend." One day, I only know,
The vague companionship that I'd seen grow
So imperceptibly, turned gold, and ran
In tune with all I'd thought or dared to plan.
Since then, you've been to me like music, low,
Yet clear; a fire that throws its warm, bright
    glow
On me as on each woman, child, and man,
And common thing that lies within its rays;
You've been like wholesome food that stays
    the cry
Of hungry, groping minds; and like a star—
A self-sufficient star—you make me raise
My utmost being to a higher sky,
In tune, like you, with earth, yet wide, and far.

—Florence Steigerwalt

The Love of a Friend

Friendship–Like music heard on the waters,
Like pines when the wind passeth by,
Like pearls in the depths of the ocean,
Like stars that enamel the sky,
Like June and the odor of roses,
Like dew and the freshness of morn,
Like sunshine that kisseth the clover,
Like tassels of silk on the corn,
Like mountains that arch the blue heavens,
Like clouds when the sun dippeth low,
Like songs of birds in the forest,
Like brooks where the sweet waters flow,
Like dreams of Arcadian pleasures,
Like colors that gratefully blend,
Like everything breathing of kindness,
Like these is the love of a friend.

—A.P. STANLEY

The Friendly Things

Oh, it's just the little homely things,
The unobtrusive, friendly things,
The "Won't-you-let-me-help-you" things
That make our pathway light.
The "Laugh-with-me-it's-funny" things
And it's the jolly, joking things,
The "Never-mind-the-trouble" things,
That makes the world seem bright.
For all the countless famous things
The wondrous record-breaking things,
These "never-can-be-equaled" things
That all the papers cite.
Are not the little human things,
The "everyday encountered" things,
The "just-because-I-like-you" things,
That make us happy quite.
So here's to all the little things,
The "done-and-then-forgotten" things,
Those "oh-its-simply-nothing" things
That make life worth the fight.

—AUTHOR UNKNOWN

By Being Yourself

I LOVE YOU, not only for what you are,
But for what I am when I am with you.
I LOVE YOU, not only for what you
   have made of yourself,
But for what
You are making of me.
I LOVE YOU for the part of me
   that you bring out;
I love you
For putting your hand
Into my heaped-up heart
And passing over
All the foolish, weak things
That you can't help
Dimly seeing there,
And for drawing out
Into the light
All the beautiful belongings
That no one else has looked
Quite far enough to find.

I LOVE YOU because
You are helping to make
Of the lumber of my life
Not a tavern but a temple;
Out of the works of my every day
Not a reproach but a song.
I LOVE YOU
Because you have done
More than any creed
Could have done
To make me good,
And more than any fate
Could have done
To make me happy.
You have done it by being yourself.
Perhaps that is what being a friend means,
After all.

—ROY CROFT

True Beat of Our Heart

What is the best a friend can be
To any soul, to you or me?
Not only shelter, comfort, rest—
Inmost refreshment unexpressed;
Not only a beloved guide
To thread life's labyrinth at our side,
Or with love's torch lead on before;
Though these be much, there yet is more.

The best friend is an atmosphere
Warm with all inspirations dear,
Wherein we breathe the large, free breath
Of life that hath no taint of death.
Our friend is an unconscious PART OF EVERY
TRUE BEAT OF OUR HEART;
A strength, a growth, whence we derive
Feelings that keep the world alive.

A Precious Part Of Me

"I am a part of all whom I have met,"
So, friend of mine, you are a wholesome part;
Our precious visits, lingering with me yet,
Are flowers in the garden of my heart.

Your smiles like violets, sweet beyond compare,
Your words, carnations, cheering on my way,
Your deeds like roses, rich with perfume rare,
Bring faith and hope and love every day.

So, friend of mine, though you are far away,
Between us may stretch mountain, plain,
*   or sea,*
Yet by my side you walk and talk each day,
Because you are a precious part of me.

—CHARLES ELMER CHAPLER

A Page More Glowing

If stores of dry and learned lore we gain,
We keep them in the memory of the brain:

Names, things and facts—
  whate'er we knowledge call,
There is the common ledger for them all;

And images on this cold surface traced
Make slight impressions, and are soon effaced.

But we've a page more glowing and more bright
On which our friendship and our love we write;

That these may never from the soul depart,
We trust them to the memory of the heart.

There is no dimming, no effacement there;
Each new pulsation keeps the record clear;

Warm, golden letters all the tablet fill,
Nor lose their luster till the heart stands still.

—DANIEL WEBSTER

CHAPTER 8

The Blessings of Friendship

*T*HERE ARE FRIENDS who are to us like a great rock in a weary land. We flee to them in the heat of parching days and rest in their shadow. A friend in whom we can confide without fear of disappointment; who, we are sure, will never fail us, will never stint his love in serving us, who always has healing tenderness of the hurt of our heart, comfort for our sorrow, and cheer for our discouragement, such a friend is not only a rock of shelter to us in time of danger, but is also as rivers of water in a thirsty land, when our hearts cry out for life and love.

–J. R. MILLER

It is my joy in life to find
At every turning of the road
The strong arms of a comrade kind
To help me onward with my load;
And since I have no gold to give,
And love alone must make amends,
My only prayer is, while I live–
GOD MAKE ME WORTHY
OF MY FRIENDS.

–FRANK DEMPSTER SHERMAN

A Friend in Need

"A friend in need," my neighbor said to me—
    "A friend indeed is what I mean to be;
In time of trouble I will come to you
    And in the hour of need you'll find me
      true."

I thought a bit, and took him by the hand;
    "My friend," said I,
      "you do not understand
The inner meaning of that simple rhyme—
    A friend is what the heart needs
    all the time."

—HENRY VAN DYKE

Friend! How sacred the word. Born in the heart of God, and given to man as a treasure from the eternities—no word in the languages so heavily freighted with meaning.

With one friend I would count myself rich; to possess more than one, I were rich beyond comparison. A friend is a priceless gem for the crown of life here and a cherished star in memory forever.

—CYRUS B. NUBBAUM

The Language of Friendship

Friendship takes place between those who have an affinity for one another, and is a perfectly natural and inevitable result. No professions or advances will avail. Even speech, at first, necessarily has nothing to do with it; but it follows after silence, as the buds in the graft do not put forth into leaves till long after the graft has taken. It is a drama in which the parties have no part to act....

Friendship is never established as an understood relation. Do you demand that I be less your friend that you may know it? Yet what right have I to think that another cherishes so rare a sentiment for me? It is a miracle which requires constant proofs. It is an exercise of the finest imagination and the rarest faith. It says by a silent but eloquent behavior: "I will be so related to thee as thou canst not imagine; even so thou mayest believe, I will spend truth, all my wealth on thee," and the friend responds silently through his nature, and life, and treats his friend with the same divine courtesy....

The language of friendship is not words but meaning. It is an intelligence above language.

—HENRY DAVID THOREAU

The Things I Prize

These are the things I prize
And hold of dearest worth:
Light of the sapphire skies,
Peace of the silent hills,
Shelter of the forests, comfort of the grass,
Music of birds, murmurs of little rills,
Shadows of clouds that swiftly pass,
And, after showers,
The smell of flowers
And of the good brown earth,—
And best of all, along the way,
    friendship and mirth.

                     —HENRY VAN DYKE

So shall a friendship fill each heart
    With perfume sweet as roses are,
That even though we be apart,
    We'll scent the fragrance from afar.

                     —GEORGIA McCOY

For the Love of a Friend

O, for the love of a friend whose voice and touch will rainbow sorrows, diamond tears, making of them gems of rarest joy; one who forgives all my shortages ere asked to do so; one who dares to the uttermost of human imagery; one whose ship will cast anchor, and throw out the life line of hope when storms are near; one who forgives in me all that I can forgive in myself. O, for the love of a friend who can be made the sacred trustee of my heart; one who is more to me than the closest relative; one whose very name is so sacred that I want to whisper it softly; one who lingers near my door in time of distress, and stretches forth his hand, which is not empty or cold, and who says little, but feels largely.

—MAE LAWSON

CHAPTER 9

Divine Gems

To him that is afflicted,
pity should be showed from his friend.
—JOB 6:14

A friend loveth at all times,
and a brother is born for adversity.
—PROVERBS 17:17

A man that hath friends must show himself
friendly: and there is a friend that sticketh
closer than a brother.
—PROVERBS 18:24

Faithful are the wounds of a friend;
but the kisses of an enemy are deceitful.
—PROVERBS 27:6

Thine own friend, and thy father's
friend, forsake not.
—PROVERBS 27:10